Tech Made Simple

A Beginner's Guide to Digital Mastery

Tech Trends

Tech Made Simple

TABLE OF CONTENTS

Tech Made Simple

Introduction: Mastering Technology in the Digital Age

In today's fast-paced world, technology touches nearly every aspect of our lives. From the moment we wake up and check our phones, to the way we communicate, work, and entertain ourselves, technology plays a central role. However, the rapidly evolving nature of tech can make it difficult to keep up, even for the most tech-savvy among us. Whether you're a student trying to optimise your computer for schoolwork, a professional seeking to boost productivity, or someone just looking to get the most out of their gadgets, this book is here to help you master the essentials of technology in the digital age.

Why Tech Tips Matter

Efficiency and Productivity:

Technology, when used effectively, has the potential to greatly enhance our efficiency and productivity. Imagine trying to accomplish a task on your computer or smartphone without knowing the shortcuts or the most useful apps. You could end up wasting hours on something that could have been done in minutes. Knowing how to optimise your devices allows you to streamline tasks, automate repetitive actions, and make the most of the tools at your disposal. This translates to more time spent on the things that really matter—whether that's finishing a work project, studying for exams, or simply relaxing.

Digital Literacy:

In today's world, being digitally literate is no longer an option—it's a necessity. Understanding how to navigate digital spaces, from social media to cloud computing, has become as essential as knowing how to read and write. Digital literacy enables you to communicate more effectively, work more efficiently, and even safeguard your personal information from cyber threats. The more you know about technology, the more control you have over your own digital experiences.

Security and Privacy:
One of the most important reasons to familiarise yourself with tech tips is security. Cybersecurity threats are more prevalent than ever, and hackers continuously devise new ways to exploit weaknesses in systems and personal devices. By knowing the basics of protecting your devices—such as using two-factor authentication, strong passwords, and up-to-date antivirus software—you can significantly reduce your vulnerability to cyber-attacks. Moreover, understanding how to manage privacy settings on social media, browsers, and apps gives you greater control over who sees your data.

Staying Current in a Rapidly Evolving World:

Technology is constantly evolving, with new apps, tools, and devices being introduced at a dizzying pace. Staying up-to-date with these changes can feel overwhelming, but it's also crucial. As technology becomes more advanced, new ways of doing things emerge, offering opportunities to improve our daily lives. Mastering tech tips allows you to stay ahead, ensuring you're not left behind in a world that is increasingly defined by digital innovation.

How This Book Will Help You

A Comprehensive Guide for All Skill Levels: Whether you're a complete beginner or someone with moderate experience in technology, this book is designed to meet your needs. We break down complex tech concepts into simple, actionable steps. You don't need to be a tech genius to understand or implement these tips; they're written with clarity and simplicity in mind. From setting up your devices correctly to troubleshooting common problems, you'll find guidance here for every level of user.

Practical, Real-World Tips:

Every tip in this book is designed to be practical and applicable to everyday situations. Whether it's learning how to organise your desktop for better productivity or discovering how to fix your slow Wi-Fi connection, we focus on real-world scenarios that you'll likely encounter. By the end of each chapter, you'll walk away with a set of skills you can put into practice immediately.

Step-by-Step Instructions:

We don't just tell you *what* to do—we show you *how* to do it. Each section includes detailed, step-by-step instructions so you can follow along and apply the tips directly to your devices. These instructions are supplemented with illustrations and screenshots to ensure you're never left wondering if you're doing something correctly.

Focus on Security and Privacy:

In addition to helping you maximise productivity, this book emphasises the importance of keeping your digital life secure. Each chapter includes security tips tailored to the subject at hand. From learning how to create strong passwords to understanding how to spot phishing attempts, you'll be better equipped to navigate the digital world with confidence and safety.

Updated for the Latest Trends and Tools:
The world of technology never stays still, and neither does this book. We've taken into account the latest trends, from the rise of artificial intelligence (AI) tools to the growing use of smart home devices. The tools and tips you'll find here are relevant to the technology landscape as it stands today, ensuring you're well-prepared for the current digital era.

Key Terms You Should Know

Before we dive into the more advanced tips, it's helpful to clarify a few key terms that will frequently appear throughout this book. Understanding these will help you navigate the content more easily and get the most out of the tips and techniques we'll be discussing.

1. **Operating System (OS):**
   The software that manages a computer's hardware and software resources. Popular operating systems include Windows, macOS, Linux, iOS, and Android. The OS is essentially the backbone of any device, allowing you to interact with the system and run applications.

2. **App (Application):**
   An app is a software program designed to perform specific tasks, such as word processing, gaming, or communication. Apps can be installed on your smartphone, tablet, or computer, and they are often downloaded from app stores (like Google Play or the Apple App Store).

3. **Cloud Storage:**
   A service that allows you to store data (documents, photos, videos, etc.) on remote servers, which can be accessed via the internet. Examples include Google Drive, iCloud, and Dropbox. Cloud storage offers the convenience of accessing your files from anywhere and

on any device, as long as you're connected to the internet.

4. **Antivirus Software:**

   A program designed to detect, prevent, and remove malware (viruses, spyware, etc.) from your devices. Using antivirus software is crucial for protecting your personal information and ensuring your devices run smoothly.

5. **Wi-Fi:**

   Wireless technology that allows devices like smartphones, laptops, and tablets to connect to the internet or communicate with one another without the need for physical cables. Wi-Fi is a fundamental part of modern technology and enables most of our daily digital activities.

6. **Two-Factor Authentication (2FA):**

   A security process that requires two forms of identification before you can access an account or system. For example, after entering your password, you might be asked to enter a code sent to your phone.

2FA adds an extra layer of security to your online accounts.

7. **Browser:**

A browser is software that allows you to access and navigate the internet. Popular browsers include Google Chrome, Mozilla Firefox, Safari, and Microsoft Edge. Browsers also provide tools to help you manage your online activity, such as bookmarks and extensions.

8. **Bandwidth:**

Bandwidth refers to the amount of data that can be transmitted over an internet connection in a specific amount of time. The higher your bandwidth, the faster your internet connection. Understanding bandwidth can help you troubleshoot slow internet speeds or choose the right internet plan for your needs.

9. **Phishing:**

A type of cyber-attack where hackers attempt to steal personal information by disguising themselves as legitimate entities through emails, messages, or websites. Phishing attacks often trick users into clicking malicious links or providing sensitive data.

Chapter 1: Setting Up Your Devices for Success

Setting up your devices correctly is the foundation of a smooth and productive tech experience. Whether you're using a smartphone, tablet, or laptop, a well-organised device not only improves efficiency but also helps prevent common frustrations like slow performance or data loss. In this chapter, we'll walk you through the essential steps to set up your devices for success—from configuring basic settings and optimising performance to selecting key apps and securing your digital life with antivirus and backup strategies.

Getting Started with Smartphones, Tablets, and Laptops

The first time you unbox a new device, it can feel like stepping into a new world. While it's exciting, the setup process is crucial to ensuring you get the most out of your device from the start. Whether you're working with a smartphone, tablet, or laptop, there are universal steps that help you establish a strong foundation.

Smartphones and Tablets

1. **Account Setup (Apple ID, Google Account, Microsoft Account):**
   The very first step in setting up a smartphone or tablet is creating or logging into your main account (Apple ID for iOS, Google Account for Android, or Microsoft Account for Windows devices). These accounts allow you to sync data, download apps, and access cloud services. If you're setting up multiple devices, having the same account across devices ensures seamless integration and syncing.

22

2. **Wi-Fi Connection and Updates:**
   As soon as your device is turned on, connecting it to a stable Wi-Fi network is essential. This will allow the device to check for software updates. Updating your device's operating system (OS) ensures that you have the latest features, security patches, and bug fixes.

3. **Personalization Settings (Language, Date, Time, Display):**
   During the initial setup, you'll be prompted to choose your language, region, and other basic settings such as display preferences (light or dark mode) and font sizes. These personalization settings can be adjusted later, but it's good to configure them early on to suit your preferences and make your device easier to use.

4. **Apps and Notifications:**
   Once you're logged in and connected to Wi-Fi, it's time to download essential apps. Depending on the platform, you can do this via the App Store (iOS) or Google

Play Store (Android). To avoid being overwhelmed by alerts, managing your notification preferences right away is a smart move. You can choose which apps can send you notifications and how frequently.

5. **Cloud Services (iCloud, Google Drive, OneDrive):**
Cloud storage is invaluable for backing up important files, photos, and videos, as well as for syncing content across devices. Whether you're using iCloud, Google Drive, or OneDrive, make sure it's enabled and set up properly. This will protect your data and make it accessible from anywhere.

Laptops

Setting up a laptop shares many similarities with smartphones and tablets, but there are a few key differences to note.

1. **Install or Log Into Your Operating System (Windows, macOS, Linux):**

If your laptop comes with an OS pre-installed, you'll be asked to log in or create a new user profile. If you're installing an OS manually, make sure you follow the installation guide carefully. Once inside your OS, configuring user accounts will allow for personalised settings and data storage for each user on the device.

2. **Wi-Fi and Network Settings:**
Similar to smartphones, connecting your laptop to Wi-Fi or an Ethernet network is crucial. Check that the connection is secure, and be sure to test the speed and stability to ensure smooth performance, especially if you rely on the internet for work or school.

3. **Display and Sound Settings:**
You'll want to adjust your display resolution to optimise the visual experience, particularly if you're working with graphics, watching videos, or gaming. For sound settings, connect any external speakers, headphones, or

microphones, and test the volume levels to ensure they work correctly.

4. **Software Updates and Driver Installations:**
Right after setup, it's important to check for system updates and hardware drivers. These drivers ensure that your laptop's hardware (like the graphics card, printer, or webcam) communicates effectively with the OS. Updated drivers enhance performance and fix bugs that may cause slowdowns or crashes.

Optimising Your Computer's Performance

Even the most powerful devices can slow down over time if they're not optimised properly. Fortunately, there are several strategies you can implement to keep your computer running smoothly.

1. **Uninstall Unnecessary Programs:**
Many new laptops come with pre-installed

software, often called "bloatware," that can slow down your system. Go through your list of installed applications and uninstall any that you don't need. This will free up valuable disk space and reduce the load on your system.

2. **Limit Startup Programs:**
   Many programs automatically run when your computer starts, slowing down boot time and consuming system resources. You can manage these programs by opening your Task Manager (Windows) or Activity Monitor (macOS) and disabling non-essential apps from launching at startup.

3. **Clean Up Your Hard Drive:**
   Regularly cleaning up your hard drive improves performance. Use built-in tools like Disk Cleanup on Windows or Storage Management on macOS to delete temporary files, system cache, and unnecessary data. Additionally, organising your files into folders can help keep everything in order and reduce clutter.

4. **Optimise Your Browser:**
   Web browsers often become resource-heavy, especially when multiple tabs or extensions are in use. Clear your browser cache regularly and disable or remove unused browser extensions. Using lightweight browsers or adjusting your browser's settings can also boost performance.

5. **Upgrade Your Hardware (RAM, SSD):**
   If your laptop is still sluggish after software optimization, consider upgrading the hardware. Adding more RAM (memory) or replacing your hard drive with a Solid-State Drive (SSD) can dramatically improve your computer's speed and responsiveness.

6. **Regular Maintenance and Updates:**
   Keeping your OS and apps up to date ensures that they run efficiently and are protected against bugs and vulnerabilities. Schedule regular system maintenance, such as checking for updates, scanning for

malware, and defragmenting your hard drive (for Windows users).

Key Apps and Software Every User Needs

Regardless of your personal or professional needs, certain apps and software can improve your digital experience and productivity. Here are some essential tools every user should consider:

1. **Productivity Suite (Microsoft Office, Google Workspace, LibreOffice):** Whether you're writing documents, creating spreadsheets, or delivering presentations, a productivity suite is crucial. Microsoft Office is a popular choice, but Google Workspace offers free alternatives like Google Docs and Sheets. LibreOffice is a good open-source option.
2. **Communication Tools (Zoom, Microsoft Teams, Slack):** Video conferencing and communication

tools are essential for both personal and professional use. Zoom and Microsoft Teams allow for video calls, webinars, and virtual meetings, while Slack is perfect for team messaging and collaboration.

3. **Cloud Storage (Google Drive, Dropbox, OneDrive):**
   Cloud storage services allow you to store and access files from anywhere, making collaboration easier and providing peace of mind that your data is safely backed up. These services often come with free storage space and paid plans for additional capacity.

4. **Antivirus Software (Norton, McAfee, Avast):**
   Keeping your devices protected from malware is critical. Antivirus software scans your system for threats, monitors suspicious activity, and provides real-time protection. Some systems come with built-in antivirus (like Windows Defender), but third-party solutions may offer more comprehensive features.

5. **Media Players (VLC, Spotify, YouTube):**
   For entertainment purposes, you'll want a reliable media player. VLC is a versatile video player that handles virtually any format, while Spotify and YouTube provide access to millions of songs and videos for streaming.

6. **Password Managers (LastPass, Dashlane, 1Password):**
   With countless accounts requiring passwords, a password manager helps store and encrypt your passwords in one place. These apps also generate strong passwords for you, ensuring better security without the need to remember dozens of different combinations.

Security First: Antivirus, Passwords, and Backups

In our increasingly digital world, security should always be a top priority. From protecting your devices from viruses to safeguarding personal information with strong passwords, these are the steps you should take to secure your digital life.

1. **Antivirus Software:**
   Installing antivirus software is the first line of defence against malware, viruses, and other cyber threats. It continuously scans your device for suspicious files or activities and neutralises threats before they cause damage. Many antivirus solutions also come with firewalls and additional privacy features, offering a comprehensive security package.

2. **Creating Strong Passwords:**
   Weak passwords are one of the most common ways hackers gain access to your accounts. To secure your data, use passwords that are at least 12 characters long and combine uppercase and lowercase letters, numbers, and symbols. Avoid using personal information (like birthdays) and opt for a password manager to generate and store unique passwords for each of your accounts.

3. **Two-Factor Authentication (2FA):**
   Two-factor authentication adds an extra layer of security to your accounts. Even if a hacker obtains your password, they'll still need access to a second form of identification, such as a code sent to your phone. Whenever possible, enable 2FA for your most sensitive accounts, like email, banking, and social media.

4. **Backups (Cloud and Local):**
   Data loss can happen unexpectedly—whether from hardware failure, accidental deletion, or malware attacks like ransomware. Regular backups ensure that your important files are safe. Use a combination of cloud storage (e.g., Google Drive, iCloud, Dropbox) and external drives to back up your data. Many cloud services offer automatic backups, which add convenience to the process.

5. **Regular Security Audits:**
   It's a good idea to periodically review your security settings. Check for any

outdated passwords, disable accounts you no longer use, and monitor for any unusual activity in your online accounts. If you suspect your information has been compromised, change your passwords immediately and run a full antivirus scan on your device.

Chapter 2: Mastering the Basics of the Internet

The internet is the backbone of modern technology, providing access to vast amounts of information, communication platforms, and entertainment. Whether you're a casual user or someone who depends on the internet for work or study, understanding the basics of the internet can help you navigate it more effectively, avoid security risks, and even optimise your connection for better performance. In this chapter, we'll cover essential topics such as Wi-Fi, cellular data, browser basics, safe browsing practices, and ways to boost your internet speed.

Understanding Wi-Fi, Cellular, and Data Plans

The internet can be accessed through various types of connections, primarily via Wi-Fi and cellular data. While both provide internet access, they differ in terms of speed, cost, and availability. Understanding these differences will help you make the right choice for your needs.

Wi-Fi

Wi-Fi is a wireless networking technology that allows devices such as smartphones, laptops, tablets, and smart TVs to connect to the internet without using cables. It typically relies on a modem and router to deliver internet access to multiple devices within a specific range. Wi-Fi is common in homes, offices, cafes, and public spaces, providing high-speed internet without consuming data from a cellular plan.

1. **How Wi-Fi Works:**
   Wi-Fi transmits data using radio waves
   between your device and a router, which
   then communicates with your internet
   service provider (ISP) to access the
   internet. The range of a typical Wi-Fi
   network is around 150 feet indoors and
   300 feet outdoors, though this can vary
   depending on the quality of the router and
   the environment.

2. **Public vs. Private Wi-Fi Networks:**
   Private Wi-Fi networks are secured with
   passwords and are typically found in
   homes and offices. Public Wi-Fi, on the
   other hand, is available in places like
   cafes, libraries, and airports. While
   convenient, public networks can be less
   secure, making your data more vulnerable
   to cyberattacks. Always use caution when
   accessing sensitive information on public
   Wi-Fi.

3. **Choosing the Right Router:**
   The router you use plays a big role in the
   quality of your Wi-Fi connection.

Consider factors like range, speed, and security features when purchasing a router. Dual-band routers that operate on both 2.4GHz and 5GHz frequencies are generally better for reducing congestion and improving speed.

Cellular Data

Cellular data is internet access provided by your mobile carrier. It allows you to connect to the internet anywhere your phone gets a signal, even when Wi-Fi is unavailable. Cellular data comes in various forms, from 3G and 4G to the faster 5G, with different plans and pricing models.

1. **How Cellular Data Works:**
   Cellular data uses your mobile carrier's network to connect to the internet, transmitting data over the same towers that handle phone calls. Unlike Wi-Fi, cellular data works in more remote locations, though it's often more limited by data caps and speed throttling based on your plan.

2. **Understanding Data Plans (Prepaid vs. Postpaid):**
   Cellular data plans vary widely depending on your carrier and country. Prepaid plans allow you to pay for data upfront without a contract, while postpaid plans often include a set amount of data per month with overage fees if you exceed your limit. Unlimited data plans are available, but they may come with speed restrictions after reaching a certain usage threshold.

3. **Monitoring Data Usage:**
   Keeping an eye on your data usage is crucial, especially if you have a limited plan. Most smartphones have built-in features that track data usage. Regularly monitoring your usage helps avoid overage fees and ensures you stay within your plan's limits.

4. **Hotspots:**
   Some smartphones can act as Wi-Fi hotspots, allowing other devices to connect to the internet using your cellular data. This feature is particularly useful

when Wi-Fi isn't available, but it can consume a significant amount of data, so use it carefully.

Browser Basics: Chrome, Firefox, Safari, and Edge

Browsers are your gateway to the internet. Whether you're researching information, checking email, or shopping online, browsers allow you to access websites and online content. Let's break down the basics of the most popular browsers: Chrome, Firefox, Safari, and Edge.

Google Chrome

1. **Features and Performance:**
   Google Chrome is one of the most widely used browsers due to its speed, clean interface, and integration with Google services. It offers a variety of features such as tab management, an extensive library of extensions, and synchronisation across devices via your Google account.
2. **Pros and Cons:**

- ○ *Pros*: Fast, user-friendly, extensive extension support.
- ○ *Cons*: Can be resource-heavy, consuming significant memory (RAM), which may slow down your device.

3. **Best Uses:**
   Chrome is ideal for users heavily invested in the Google ecosystem, offering seamless integration with services like Gmail, Google Docs, and Google Drive.

Mozilla Firefox

1. **Features and Performance:**
   Firefox is known for its emphasis on privacy and security, offering features such as enhanced tracking protection and customizable privacy settings. It also provides a wide array of extensions and is more lightweight than Chrome, making it a great choice for users with lower-powered devices.

2. **Pros and Cons:**

- ○ *Pros*: Strong privacy features, less resource-heavy than Chrome.
- ○ *Cons*: Slightly slower than Chrome in terms of loading speed.

3. **Best Uses:**
Firefox is a strong choice for users who prioritise privacy and want a customizable browsing experience.

Safari

1. **Features and Performance:**
Safari is Apple's default browser for macOS and iOS devices. It's optimised for Apple hardware, providing excellent performance and battery efficiency on MacBooks, iPhones, and iPads. Safari offers features like Reader Mode, which simplifies web pages for easier reading, and a built-in ad blocker.

2. **Pros and Cons:**
- ○ *Pros*: Optimised for Apple devices, energy-efficient, fast performance.

      o   *Cons*: Limited customization options and extensions compared to Chrome and Firefox.

3. **Best Uses:**
Safari is perfect for Apple users who want a fast and efficient browsing experience that's integrated with their devices.

Microsoft Edge

1. **Features and Performance:**
Edge, now based on the same Chromium engine as Chrome, has greatly improved in recent years. It offers fast browsing speeds, solid security features, and a streamlined design. Microsoft Edge also provides built-in features like a PDF reader and the ability to save web pages for offline use.

2. **Pros and Cons:**
      o   *Pros*: Lightweight, fast, integrated with Windows 10 and 11 features like Cortana.
      o   *Cons*: Fewer extensions compared to Chrome.

3. **Best Uses:**
   Edge is ideal for Windows users looking for a lightweight, fast browser that integrates well with Microsoft services.

Safe Browsing Tips: Avoiding Scams and Phishing

While the internet is a valuable tool, it also has risks. Scammers and cybercriminals are constantly developing new ways to trick users into giving up personal information or installing malware. Safe browsing practices are essential to protect yourself from these threats.

Recognizing Phishing Scams

1. **What is Phishing?**
   Phishing is a type of cyberattack where attackers impersonate legitimate companies or individuals to trick users into revealing personal information, such as passwords or credit card details. This is often done via email, text messages, or

fake websites that closely resemble the real ones.

2. **How to Spot Phishing Emails:**
   o Check the sender's email address: Phishing emails often come from addresses that look similar to official ones but contain minor differences (e.g., support@paypaI.com instead of support@paypal.com).
   o Look for generic greetings: Legitimate companies often address you by name, while phishing emails tend to use generic greetings like "Dear Customer."
   o Beware of urgent language: Phishing emails often create a sense of urgency, saying things like "Your account will be suspended unless you act now."

3. **Avoiding Phishing Links:**
   Always hover over links in emails before clicking them. The URL that appears

should match the legitimate website. If something looks suspicious, don't click it.

Safe Browsing Habits

1. **Use Secure Websites (HTTPS):**
   Ensure that the websites you visit use HTTPS, which provides an encrypted connection between your browser and the website. You can tell if a site is secure by looking for a padlock icon in the address bar.

2. **Enable Two-Factor Authentication (2FA):**
   For important accounts, like email and banking, enable 2FA to add an extra layer of protection. This makes it harder for hackers to access your accounts even if they have your password.

3. **Avoid Public Wi-Fi for Sensitive Transactions:**
   Avoid entering sensitive information like banking details or passwords when using public Wi-Fi networks. If you must, use a

Virtual Private Network (VPN) to encrypt your data.

Boosting Your Internet Speed

A slow internet connection can be frustrating, especially when trying to stream videos, download files, or participate in video calls. Here are several tips to help boost your internet speed.

1. Upgrade Your Internet Plan

Your internet speed largely depends on the plan you've subscribed to with your Internet Service Provider (ISP). If you frequently experience slow speeds, it may be time to upgrade to a faster plan with higher bandwidth.

2. Optimise Your Wi-Fi Setup

1. **Router Placement:**
   The placement of your router can significantly affect the strength of your Wi-Fi signal. Place your router in a central location, away from walls and

obstructions, for the best coverage. Avoid placing it near metal objects or electronic devices that could interfere with the signal.

2. **Use a Wi-Fi Extender:**
   If you have a large home or weak signal in certain areas, consider using a Wi-Fi extender or mesh network system to improve coverage.

3. Reduce Bandwidth Usage

If multiple devices are using the internet simultaneously (e.g., streaming video, downloading files, or gaming), it can slow down your connection. To improve speed, limit the number of devices or activities using the internet at the same time.

4. Clear Browser Cache

Over time, your browser's cache—temporary data stored to speed up page loading—can slow down your internet experience. Regularly clearing your cache can improve speed and performance.

5. Use Ethernet for Faster Speeds

While Wi-Fi is convenient, a wired Ethernet connection is often faster and more stable. If you're experiencing slow speeds during activities like gaming or video conferencing, consider connecting your device directly to the router with an Ethernet cable.

6. Restart Your Router Regularly

Like most tech devices, routers can benefit from a reboot now and then. Restarting your router clears temporary issues and can refresh your connection to your ISP.

Chapter 3: Troubleshooting Common Tech Problems

Technology is an integral part of modern life, but even the most advanced devices can experience issues. Whether you're dealing with a sluggish computer, connectivity problems, or constant software crashes, understanding how to troubleshoot these common tech issues is essential for maintaining productivity and reducing frustration.

Slow Devices: What's Slowing You Down?

A device that once ran smoothly but is now lagging can be incredibly frustrating. Whether it's your smartphone, tablet, or computer, the culprit behind a slow device can be related to hardware limitations, software issues, or insufficient storage. Let's dive into some of the common reasons devices slow down and how to fix them.

1. Too Many Background Processes

One of the most common causes of slow devices is having too many background processes running simultaneously. These are apps or programs that continue to run even when you're not actively using them, consuming memory (RAM) and processing power.

- **How to Check Background Processes on Computers:**
  For Windows users, press *Ctrl + Shift + Esc* to open Task Manager, and for Mac users, go to *Activity Monitor* (found in Applications > Utilities). Here, you can see all running processes and how much

CPU and memory they are using. Closing
unnecessary processes can significantly
boost performance.

- **For Smartphones:**
On Android devices, go to *Settings >
Apps > Running Apps*, and on iPhones,
double-tap the home button (or swipe up
from the bottom of the screen on newer
models) to see running apps. Swipe away
any apps you're not using.

2. Insufficient Storage

If your device's storage is full or nearly full, it
can slow down performance. Operating systems
need free space to perform tasks like
downloading updates, caching files, and running
applications efficiently.

- **Freeing Up Storage on Smartphones:**
Go to your device's storage settings to see
what's taking up the most space. Delete
old apps, photos, videos, and unused files
to free up room. You can also use cloud
storage options like Google Drive, iCloud,

or OneDrive to offload large files without losing access to them.

- **Freeing Up Storage on Computers:** Delete unnecessary files such as old downloads, temporary files, and unused programs. On Windows, use the *Disk Cleanup* tool, and on Macs, go to *About This Mac > Storage* and click on "Manage" for suggestions on optimising storage.

3. Outdated Software

Software updates are designed to fix bugs, improve performance, and add new features. If your device is running outdated software, it may slow down as it tries to manage modern apps with outdated tools.

- **Check for Software Updates:** Regularly check for system and app updates. For smartphones, you can find this option in *Settings > Software Update*. On computers, go to *Windows Update* or

53

System Preferences > Software Update for Mac.

4. Malware or Viruses

Malware and viruses can cause significant performance issues. These malicious programs run in the background, consuming your device's resources and even stealing data.

- **How to Fix It:**
  Run a full scan using a reputable antivirus or anti-malware tool. If malware is detected, follow the program's instructions to remove it. Regular scans help keep your device safe and running efficiently.

Connectivity Issues: Fixing Wi-Fi and Network Problems

Losing internet connectivity can be frustrating, especially if you rely on it for work, streaming, or communication. Wi-Fi and network issues are common, but with the right approach, they can often be resolved quickly.

1. Weak Wi-Fi Signal

A weak or unstable Wi-Fi signal is a common cause of connectivity problems. This can happen due to the distance from the router, interference from other devices, or obstructions like walls and floors.

- **How to Improve Wi-Fi Signal:**
  - **Move Closer to the Router:** The farther you are from the router, the weaker the signal. Try relocating your device or the router to improve the connection.
  - **Use a Wi-Fi Extender:** If you have a large home or office, a Wi-Fi extender can help boost the signal in areas far from the router.
  - **Reduce Interference:** Devices like microwaves, cordless phones, and Bluetooth gadgets can interfere

with Wi-Fi signals. Keep your router away from these devices.

2. Router Problems

Sometimes, the issue lies with the router itself. Over time, routers can experience technical glitches that affect performance.

- **How to Fix Router Issues:**
  - **Restart the Router:** The classic "turn it off and on again" works for a reason. Restarting your router can refresh the connection and resolve many issues. Unplug the router for 10 seconds, then plug it back in.
  - **Update Router Firmware:** Like any device, routers need occasional updates. Check your router's manufacturer website or login to the router's settings (often through a web browser) to see if there are any firmware updates available.

3. Incorrect Network Settings

Network settings can sometimes become misconfigured, leading to issues connecting to the internet.

- **How to Fix Network Settings Issues:**
  - **Reset Network Settings:** On smartphones, resetting network settings can often fix connectivity issues. Go to *Settings > General > Reset > Reset Network Settings*. Be aware that this will erase saved Wi-Fi passwords.
  - **Flush DNS Cache (for Computers):** If your computer is having trouble connecting to certain websites, flushing the DNS cache can help. On Windows, open Command Prompt and type /flushdns. On a Mac, open Terminal and type sudo killall -HUP mDNSResponder.

4. ISP Issues

Sometimes the problem isn't with your device, but with your internet service provider (ISP). Service outages, maintenance, or bandwidth throttling can all affect your internet speed and connectivity.

- **What to Do:**
  - **Check for Outages:** Visit your ISP's website or social media pages to see if there are any reported outages in your area.
  - **Contact Customer Support:** If the problem persists, contact your ISP's support team to see if there's an issue on their end.

How to Free Up Space on Your Devices

As we store more data on our devices, it's easy to run out of space. Whether you're trying to free up storage for new apps, files, or updates, there are several strategies to reclaim space on your smartphone, tablet, or computer.

1. Clear Cache and Temporary Files

Temporary files and cache data can accumulate over time, taking up unnecessary space.

- **Smartphones:**
  On Android, go to *Settings > Storage* and select *Cached data* to clear it. On iPhones, clearing the cache usually involves deleting and reinstalling the app that's using a lot of space.
- **Computers:**
  On Windows, use *Disk Cleanup* to delete temporary files. On Macs, use the *Optimise Storage* tool found in *About This Mac > Storage*.

2. Uninstall Unused Apps

Apps can take up a significant amount of storage, especially if you have games or media-rich apps installed.

- **Smartphones:**
  Go to *Settings > Apps* (or *Applications*) and sort by size to see which apps are

taking up the most space. Uninstall apps you no longer use.

- **Computers:**
  On Windows, go to *Control Panel > Programs > Uninstall a program* to remove unused programs. On Macs, simply drag unwanted apps to the Trash and empty it.

3. Move Files to the Cloud

Cloud storage services like Google Drive, iCloud, OneDrive, and Dropbox allow you to store files online, freeing up local storage on your device.

- **How to Use Cloud Storage:**
  Upload files, photos, and videos to the cloud and delete them from your local storage. Make sure to configure automatic backups so new files are automatically uploaded to the cloud.

4. Delete Large Files

Sometimes, large files such as videos, downloads, and backups can take up a lot of space.

- **Smartphones:**
  Go to *Settings* > *Storage* and check for large media files or apps. Consider deleting videos or transferring them to your computer or external storage.
- **Computers:**
  On both Windows and Mac, you can use file management tools to sort files by size and easily locate and delete large, unnecessary files.

Software Crashes: Quick Fixes for Apps and Programs

Few things are more frustrating than having an app or program crash right in the middle of an important task. Software crashes can be caused by a variety of issues, including bugs, insufficient memory, or conflicts with other programs. Here's how to troubleshoot and fix crashing apps.

1. Update the App or Program

Often, crashes occur because the software you're using is outdated and no longer compatible with your device's operating system.

- **How to Update:**
    - On smartphones, visit the app store (Google Play or App Store) and check for updates.
    - On computers, go to the program's website or use the built-in update checker to download the latest version.

2. Free Up Memory

Insufficient RAM (memory) can cause apps to crash, especially if multiple apps are running at once.

- **Freeing Up Memory on Smartphones:** Close background apps that you're not using. If your phone frequently crashes, consider upgrading to a device with more RAM.

- **Freeing Up Memory on Computers:**
  Close unnecessary programs and browser
  tabs. If crashes are frequent, consider
  upgrading your RAM or using a task
  manager to identify memory-hogging
  apps.

3. Reinstall the App or Program

Sometimes, reinstalling the app can solve
persistent crashing issues. Uninstall the app,
restart your device, and then reinstall it from the
app store or official website.

4. Check for Conflicting Programs

On computers, some programs may conflict with
each other, causing crashes. This is especially
common with antivirus programs or software
that accesses similar system resources.

- **How to Fix Conflicting Programs:**
  Disable or uninstall programs you suspect
  might be causing conflicts, then check if
  the issue is resolved.

5. Scan for Malware

Malware or viruses can cause programs to crash or behave erratically.

- **How to Fix It:**
  Run a virus scan using your antivirus program. If malware is detected, follow the software's instructions to remove it.

Chapter 4: Enhancing Your Productivity with Technology

In today's fast-paced digital world, leveraging technology is essential for boosting productivity, whether you're managing a hectic school schedule, balancing work projects, or juggling multiple personal tasks. From apps that streamline your workflow to cloud storage that keeps your documents accessible anywhere, modern technology offers countless tools to help you stay organised and efficient.

The Best Productivity Apps for Work and School

Productivity apps can be game-changers when it comes to organising tasks, managing time, and keeping on top of deadlines. Whether you need help with project management, note-taking, or staying focused, these apps are designed to make your life easier.

1. Project Management Apps

Project management tools help you keep track of tasks, deadlines, and progress. They are particularly useful for work teams or group projects at school, but even for personal organisation, these apps can ensure you never miss a deadline.

- **Trello**: This visual project management tool uses boards, lists, and cards to organise tasks. Each task can be moved between different stages, such as "To Do," "In Progress," and "Completed." Trello is great for individuals and teams, allowing collaboration through shared boards.

- **Asana**: A robust project management platform, Asana helps users break large projects into smaller tasks. You can assign tasks to team members, set due dates, and track the project's overall progress. Asana is ideal for group work or long-term projects.
- **Microsoft To-Do**: Simple yet effective, Microsoft To-Do helps you create and manage to-do lists. It's perfect for personal task management and offers integration with Microsoft Outlook for professionals who want to manage their work and personal tasks in one place.

2. Note-Taking and Organization Apps

Having a reliable note-taking app can improve your ability to capture important information and organise your thoughts.

- **Evernote**: One of the most popular note-taking apps, Evernote allows you to create and organise notes, add images, create to-do lists, and even attach documents. With cloud sync, your notes are available across devices.

- **Notion**: This all-in-one workspace blends note-taking, project management, and team collaboration. Notion lets you create personal dashboards, organise notes, and build databases to track projects or academic assignments.

- **Google Keep**: Ideal for quick notes, Google Keep lets you create simple text, image, or voice notes that can be accessed from any device. It's perfect for capturing ideas on the go, making lists, and setting reminders.

3. Focus and Distraction-Blocking Apps

Staying focused in a world full of digital distractions is tough. Focus apps help by blocking distracting websites or apps so you can concentrate on the task at hand.

- **Forest**: A fun focus app that helps you stay off your phone. When you want to focus, you plant a virtual tree, and the longer you focus, the bigger the tree grows. If you leave the app to check your phone, the tree withers and dies.
- **Freedom**: Freedom blocks distracting websites and apps across all your devices, allowing you to focus on work or study. You can schedule sessions in advance or start a session on-demand when you need some focused time.
- **Pomodoro Timer**: Based on the Pomodoro Technique (working in 25-minute intervals with 5-minute breaks), this app helps you manage your time and avoid burnout. It's great for breaking large tasks into manageable chunks.

Mastering Cloud Storage: Google Drive, iCloud, and Dropbox

Cloud storage has revolutionised the way we store and access files. Instead of being tied to a single device, cloud services allow you to store documents, photos, and other files online, where they can be accessed from anywhere with an internet connection. Here's how to make the most of popular cloud storage services like Google Drive, iCloud, and Dropbox.

1. Google Drive

Google Drive is one of the most widely used cloud storage platforms, offering 15 GB of free storage and seamless integration with other Google services like Docs, Sheets, and Gmail.

- **Organizing Files in Google Drive**: You can create folders to keep your files organised by category (e.g., Work, School, Personal). Use colour-coding to make important folders stand out, and remember to utilise Google's powerful search function to quickly find specific documents.

- **Collaborating in Google Drive**: Google Drive allows you to share documents with others, either as view-only or with editing permissions. Collaboration in real-time is made easy with Google Docs, Sheets, and Slides, which allow multiple people to work on a document simultaneously.
- **Backup Your Devices**: Google Drive also offers backup options for Android devices, which can automatically save photos, contacts, and app data. This ensures that your files are safe in case your device is lost or damaged.

2. iCloud

iCloud is Apple's cloud storage service, integrated with the entire Apple ecosystem, including iPhones, iPads, and MacBooks. It's especially convenient for Apple users, as it offers automatic backup of photos, documents, and device settings.

- **iCloud Storage Plans**: iCloud starts with 5 GB of free storage, but users can upgrade to paid plans for more space. It's best for backing up photos, messages, and app data, especially if you have multiple Apple devices.

- **Using iCloud Drive**: For document storage, iCloud Drive allows you to store and organise files in folders, just like on a traditional computer. These files can be accessed from any Apple device and even from Windows computers via iCloud.com.
- **Seamless Integration Across Devices**: iCloud automatically syncs your photos, contacts, calendar, and even Safari bookmarks across all Apple devices. This makes it incredibly convenient for users who work across multiple Apple platforms.

3. Dropbox

Dropbox offers a versatile cloud storage solution that works well across all platforms, including Windows, Mac, Android, and iOS.

- **Storing Files in Dropbox**: Dropbox allows you to upload and organise files in folders, and you can sync your files across all devices. This makes Dropbox ideal for people who work across different platforms or need to share files with others.
- **Dropbox Paper**: Dropbox also offers its own collaborative document-editing tool, Dropbox Paper, which lets multiple users work together in real-time, making it a great option for group projects or team-based tasks.
- **Link Sharing**: One of Dropbox's standout features is link sharing. You can easily create a shareable link for any file or folder in your Dropbox and send it to anyone, even if they don't have a Dropbox account.

Smart Use of Email: Organising and Managing Inboxes

Email is one of the most common communication tools, but managing your inbox can be overwhelming if it becomes cluttered with unread messages, spam, and important emails mixed together. Proper email management can help you stay on top of things without feeling overwhelmed.

1. Organise Your Inbox with Folders and Labels

Creating folders (or labels in Gmail) allows you to organise your emails by category. For instance, you could create folders for Work, School, Personal, and Important Emails.

- **How to Create Folders**: In most email clients, creating folders is simple. Look for options like "New Folder" or "Create Label" in your email settings. After creating the folder, drag and drop relevant emails into their respective categories.
- **Automatic Filters**: Many email clients, including Gmail and Outlook, allow you to set up automatic filters that sort

incoming emails into specific folders based on criteria like the sender's address or keywords. This helps declutter your inbox by moving less important emails out of the way.

2. Use Email Scheduling

Scheduling emails is a great way to manage communication, especially if you're working with people in different time zones or if you want to send an email at a specific time.

- **How to Schedule Emails**: Gmail, Outlook, and many other email platforms offer email scheduling as a built-in feature. After composing your email, look for an option to "Send Later" or "Schedule Send" and select the date and time you'd like the email to be sent.

3. Unsubscribe from Spam and Newsletters

If you're receiving too many promotional emails or newsletters that you no longer want, unsubscribing can drastically reduce the clutter in your inbox.

- **How to Unsubscribe**: Most promotional emails have an "Unsubscribe" link at the bottom. Clicking this will remove you from their mailing list. For a faster approach, apps like Unroll.Me can help you unsubscribe from multiple email lists in bulk.

Time Management Tools: Calendars, To-Do Lists, and More

Effectively managing your time is critical for staying productive, whether you're handling school assignments, work projects, or personal tasks. Time management tools, such as calendars and to-do list apps, can help you keep track of deadlines and maintain a balanced schedule.

1. Digital Calendars

Digital calendars are a simple but powerful tool for managing your time. They allow you to schedule appointments, set reminders, and keep track of deadlines.

- **Google Calendar**: Google Calendar integrates with your Google account, syncing across all devices and allowing you to create events, set reminders, and even share your calendar with others. One of the best features is its ability to send automatic email or mobile reminders before events.
- **Outlook Calendar**: If you use Microsoft products, Outlook Calendar integrates well with email and the Microsoft Office suite. You can schedule meetings, receive reminders, and even use the app across Windows, Mac, and mobile devices.

2. To-Do Lists and Task Managers

To-do list apps help you track your tasks, mark items as completed, and prioritise your day.

- **Todoist**: Todoist is a flexible task manager that allows you to create tasks, set deadlines, and prioritise items. You can organise tasks into projects (e.g., Work, Personal, School) and even break large tasks into subtasks for better management.

- **Microsoft To Do**: For those who prefer simplicity, Microsoft To Do offers a clean interface for managing tasks and lists. You can set deadlines and reminders and sync tasks across devices.

3. Time Tracking Tools

If you want to understand how you're spending your time and improve productivity, time-tracking apps can be valuable tools.

- **RescueTime**: RescueTime runs in the background and tracks how much time you spend on different apps or websites. It provides reports that show you where your time goes and helps you identify any time-wasting habits.
- **Toggl**: A time-tracking app popular with freelancers and students, Toggl allows you to start and stop timers for tasks. This

helps you understand how much time you spend on different activities and enables better time allocation.

Chapter 5: Tech for Personal Use and Entertainment

In our digital age, technology has significantly transformed how we entertain ourselves and manage our daily lives. From streaming services that provide on-demand access to movies and music to smart home devices that enhance our living environments, technology has become an integral part of our personal and entertainment experiences. This chapter explores various technologies that enrich our personal lives, focusing on streaming services, smart home devices, photo and video editing, and gaming optimization.

Streaming Services: Netflix, Spotify, and More

Streaming services have revolutionised how we consume media. Gone are the days of waiting for a movie to be released on DVD or purchasing individual songs. Today, platforms like Netflix and Spotify offer vast libraries of content at our fingertips, allowing us to enjoy entertainment on-demand.

1. Overview of Streaming Platforms

- **Netflix**: A pioneer in the streaming industry, Netflix offers a vast library of movies, TV shows, documentaries, and original content. Its user-friendly interface, personalised recommendations, and the ability to download content for offline viewing make it a top choice for many viewers.

- **Spotify**: As one of the leading music streaming services, Spotify provides access to millions of songs, podcasts, and curated playlists. Users can create custom playlists, follow artists, and discover new music based on their listening habits through personalised features like Discover Weekly.
- **Other Notable Services**:
    - **Amazon Prime Video**: Offers a wide variety of films and series, along with exclusive Prime Originals.
    - **Hulu**: Known for its extensive collection of current TV episodes, classic series, and original content.
    - **Disney+**: Features content from Disney, Pixar, Marvel, Star Wars, and National Geographic, making it a hit among families and fans of franchise content.

2. Maximising Your Streaming Experience

- **Choosing the Right Plan**: Most streaming services offer multiple subscription plans, varying in price, content availability, and features like ad-supported or ad-free experiences. Choose a plan that best fits your viewing habits and budget.
- **Creating Profiles**: Many streaming platforms allow users to create multiple profiles. This is especially useful for families, as it enables personalised recommendations and separate viewing histories for each user.
- **Using Subtitles and Audio Features**: To enhance your viewing experience, consider enabling subtitles or alternate audio tracks, especially for foreign films or content with heavy accents.
- **Offline Viewing**: Many services, like Netflix and Spotify, allow you to download content for offline access. This feature is beneficial for travel or times when internet access is limited.

Using Smart Home Devices: Alexa, Google Home, and Smart TVs

Smart home devices have transformed our living spaces into interconnected hubs of technology. These devices simplify daily tasks, enhance security, and improve entertainment experiences.

1. Voice Assistants: Alexa and Google Home

Voice assistants, like Amazon's Alexa and Google Assistant, allow users to control smart devices, play music, set reminders, and obtain information through voice commands.

- **Setting Up and Configuring**: To get started, you need a compatible smart speaker (like an Amazon Echo or Google Nest). After plugging in the device, download the respective app (Alexa or Google Home) to set up the device, link accounts, and customise settings.
- **Smart Home Integration**: Both Alexa and Google Assistant can control a variety of smart home devices, including lights,

thermostats, and security cameras. Brands like Philips Hue (lighting) and Nest (thermostats) offer compatibility with these assistants, allowing for seamless home automation.

- **Creating Routines**: You can set up routines to automate multiple actions with a single command. For example, a "Good Morning" routine could turn on the lights, start the coffee maker, and read the weather forecast.

2. Smart TVs

Smart TVs integrate internet capabilities with traditional television viewing, allowing access to streaming services, apps, and even web browsing.

- **Connecting to Wi-Fi**: To enjoy streaming services on your Smart TV, connect it to your home Wi-Fi network. This usually involves accessing the TV's settings menu and selecting your Wi-Fi network from the available options.

- **Installing Apps**: Most smart TVs come pre-installed with popular streaming apps like Netflix, Hulu, and YouTube. You can also download additional apps from the TV's app store, providing access to a broader range of content.
- **Screen Mirroring and Casting**: Many smart TVs support screen mirroring or casting from mobile devices. This feature allows you to display content from your smartphone or tablet on the TV, perfect for sharing photos, videos, or presentations.

Photo and Video Editing for Beginners

In an era where visual content is ubiquitous, learning basic photo and video editing skills can enhance your personal projects, whether it's sharing memories or creating professional-quality content for social media.

1. Choosing the Right Software

There are many user-friendly photo and video editing tools available, catering to beginners and advanced users alike.

- **Photo Editing Software**:
  - **Adobe Photoshop**: While a powerful tool, it can be overwhelming for beginners. For simple tasks, consider using **Photoshop Express**, a mobile version that simplifies editing features.
  - **Canva**: A web-based tool great for creating graphics and editing photos with templates and user-friendly features.
  - **GIMP**: A free, open-source alternative to Photoshop that offers a wide range of editing tools for more advanced users.
- **Video Editing Software**:
  - **iMovie**: A user-friendly option for Mac users, allowing basic video

editing with drag-and-drop functionality.

- ○ **Windows Movie Maker**: Though no longer officially supported, it is still available and offers simple video editing capabilities for Windows users.
- ○ **DaVinci Resolve**: A free option that provides a more advanced video editing experience, perfect for those looking to explore deeper editing features.

2. Basic Editing Techniques

- **Photo Editing**:
  - ○ **Cropping and Resizing**: Start with basic adjustments like cropping images to improve composition and resizing for optimal sharing on social media.
  - ○ **Adjusting Brightness and Contrast**: Tweak brightness and contrast to enhance the overall quality of your images. Most

editing software provides simple sliders for these adjustments.

- ○ **Applying Filters**: Experiment with filters to create a desired aesthetic. However, use filters sparingly to maintain the integrity of the original image.
- **Video Editing**:
  - ○ **Trimming Clips**: Remove unwanted sections from your videos by trimming clips to keep only the best parts. This can greatly enhance the flow of your content.
  - ○ **Adding Transitions**: Use transitions between clips to create a seamless viewing experience. Popular options include fades, wipes, and dissolves.
  - ○ **Incorporating Music and Sound Effects**: Background music can set the tone for your video. Many editing platforms offer built-in music libraries or allow you to import your own tracks.

Gaming Tips: Optimising Performance and Reducing Lag

Gaming has become one of the most popular forms of entertainment, with millions of players worldwide. However, nothing is more frustrating than lagging gameplay. Optimising your gaming setup can ensure a smooth experience.

1. Hardware Optimization

- **Upgrading Your PC**: If you're gaming on a PC, consider upgrading key components, such as the GPU (Graphics Processing Unit) and RAM (Random Access Memory). A better GPU enhances graphics quality, while additional RAM can improve multitasking capabilities.
- **Cooling Systems**: Proper cooling is essential for maintaining performance during long gaming sessions. Consider installing additional fans or using liquid cooling systems to keep temperatures down and prevent overheating.

2. Internet Connectivity

- **Wired vs. Wireless**: For online gaming, a wired Ethernet connection is often more stable than Wi-Fi, reducing latency and connection drops. If you must use Wi-Fi, ensure your router is close to your gaming device and consider using a dual-band router for better performance.
- **Reducing Bandwidth Usage**: Limit other devices on your network during gaming sessions. Streaming videos, downloading large files, or even other devices on the same network can significantly impact your gaming performance.

3. In-Game Settings

- **Adjusting Graphics Settings**: Lowering graphics settings can improve performance, especially if your hardware is not top-of-the-line. Experiment with settings like texture quality, shadow quality, and resolution to find the right balance between visuals and performance.

- **Frame Rate Optimization**: Ensure your game runs at a consistent frame rate (FPS). Some games allow you to cap the FPS to match your monitor's refresh rate, which can help reduce screen tearing and stuttering.
- **Disable Background Applications**: Close unnecessary applications running in the background that may consume resources. This includes web browsers, file-sharing apps, and other non-essential programs.

Chapter 6: Boosting Your Digital Security and Privacy

In our interconnected world, where much of our personal and financial information is stored online, safeguarding our digital security and privacy is more critical than ever. With increasing incidents of cyberattacks, identity theft, and privacy invasions, understanding how to protect ourselves online is paramount.

Understanding Two-Factor Authentication

Two-factor authentication (2FA) is a security measure that adds an additional layer of protection beyond just a username and password. By requiring two forms of identification before granting access to an account, 2FA significantly reduces the likelihood of unauthorised access.

1. How 2FA Works

- **Something You Know**: The first factor is usually your password or PIN, which is something only you should know.
- **Something You Have**: The second factor typically involves a physical device, such as a smartphone or hardware token. This can take various forms:
  - **SMS or Email Codes**: After entering your password, you may receive a code via SMS or email that you must input to access your account.

- ○ **Authenticator Apps**: Apps like Google Authenticator or Authy generate time-sensitive codes that change every 30 seconds. This method is generally more secure than SMS, as it does not rely on your mobile network.
- ○ **Biometric Identification**: Some services allow you to use fingerprint recognition or facial recognition as a second factor.

2. Setting Up 2FA

- **Enabling 2FA**: Most online services, including email providers, social media platforms, and banking sites, offer 2FA as an option. To enable it, go to the security settings of your account and follow the prompts to set it up.
- **Backup Codes**: When setting up 2FA, many services provide backup codes that you can use if you lose access to your second factor. Store these codes in a safe

place, such as a password manager or a secure location offline.

3. Benefits of 2FA

Implementing 2FA can significantly enhance your account security by:

- Reducing the risk of unauthorised access even if your password is compromised.
- Providing peace of mind, knowing that your accounts are better protected against potential threats.

How to Identify and Avoid Malware

Malware, short for malicious software, is any software designed to harm, exploit, or otherwise compromise a computer system. Understanding how to identify and avoid malware is crucial for maintaining your digital security.

1. Types of Malware

- **Viruses**: Programs that attach themselves to legitimate files and spread when the infected file is shared.
- **Worms**: Self-replicating malware that spreads across networks without needing to attach to files.
- **Trojan Horses**: Malicious software disguised as legitimate software, tricking users into installing it.
- **Spyware**: Software that secretly monitors user activity, often collecting sensitive information.
- **Ransomware**: Malware that locks or encrypts files and demands payment for access.

2. Recognizing Signs of Malware

- **Slow Performance**: If your device is suddenly slow or unresponsive, it could indicate a malware infection.
- **Unexpected Pop-Ups**: Frequent, unsolicited pop-up ads or messages can signal adware or spyware.

- **Unfamiliar Programs**: Discovering unfamiliar programs installed on your device may suggest a malware infection.
- **Browser Changes**: Unexpected changes to your web browser's homepage or search engine settings could indicate malware.

3. Strategies for Avoiding Malware

- **Install Antivirus Software**: A reputable antivirus program can help detect and remove malware. Keep it updated to ensure you have the latest protection.
- **Be Wary of Email Attachments**: Avoid opening attachments or clicking links in emails from unknown senders, as they may contain malware.
- **Download from Trusted Sources**: Only download software and applications from reputable sources or official websites to minimise the risk of malware.
- **Keep Software Updated**: Regularly update your operating system, software,

and apps to patch security vulnerabilities that malware can exploit.

Managing Privacy Settings on Social Media

Social media platforms are great for connecting with others, but they can also pose significant privacy risks if not managed correctly. Understanding how to navigate privacy settings is essential for protecting your personal information.

1. Importance of Privacy Settings

Privacy settings allow you to control who can see your posts, access your information, and contact you. Properly configuring these settings can help you maintain control over your digital footprint.

2. Key Privacy Settings to Review

- **Profile Visibility**: Determine who can view your profile and posts. Set your profile to "Friends Only" or "Private" to limit access to your connections.

- **Post Settings**: Configure your settings to control who can see your posts. Consider limiting visibility to "Friends Only" or customising audiences for specific posts.
- **Friend Requests**: Adjust settings to control who can send you friend requests. Restricting this to "Friends of Friends" or customising it can help prevent unwanted connections.
- **Location Sharing**: Be cautious about sharing your location. Disable location services for social media apps, especially when posting photos or updates.
- **Third-Party Apps**: Regularly review and revoke access for third-party apps that may have access to your social media accounts. These apps can compromise your privacy if not managed carefully.

Secure Your Online Banking and Shopping Experience

As online banking and shopping become increasingly popular, securing these transactions is essential to protect your financial information from theft and fraud.

1. Using Strong Passwords

- **Create Unique Passwords**: Use strong, unique passwords for each of your banking and shopping accounts. Avoid using easily guessable information, like birthdays or names.
- **Password Managers**: Consider using a password manager to securely store and generate complex passwords, making it easier to maintain unique passwords across different sites.

2. Look for Secure Connections

- **Check for HTTPS**: Always ensure that the website's URL begins with "https://" instead of "http://". The "s" indicates that the connection is secure and encrypted, protecting your data during transmission.

- **Avoid Public Wi-Fi**: Avoid conducting banking or shopping transactions over public Wi-Fi networks, as they can be insecure. If necessary, use a virtual private network (VPN) for added security.

3. Monitor Your Accounts Regularly

- **Review Statements**: Regularly check your bank and credit card statements for unauthorised transactions. Report any suspicious activity to your financial institution immediately.
- **Enable Alerts**: Set up transaction alerts through your bank or credit card provider to receive notifications for any account activity. This can help you quickly spot and respond to unauthorised transactions.

Chapter 7: Social Media and Communication Tips

In an increasingly digital world, social media and online communication have become essential tools for connecting with others, sharing ideas, and conducting business. However, navigating these platforms effectively requires understanding their nuances, managing distractions, and employing proper etiquette.

Navigating Social Media Platforms: Facebook, Instagram, TikTok

Social media platforms serve different purposes and attract diverse user demographics. Understanding how to navigate these platforms can enhance your online experience and help you engage with others more effectively.

1. Facebook

- **Profile and Page Setup**: Create a personal profile for connecting with friends and family, and consider setting up a public page for business or public figures. Ensure your profile picture and cover photo reflect your personality or brand.

- **Engaging with Content**: Facebook is built on interaction. Like, comment, and share posts to engage with your network. Be mindful of sharing content that aligns with your values and interests.

- **Privacy Settings**: Regularly review your privacy settings to control who can see your posts and personal information. Use the audience selector to manage visibility on individual posts.

2. Instagram

- **Visual Storytelling**: Instagram focuses on visual content. Use high-quality images and videos to convey your message. Utilise features like stories, reels, and IGTV to diversify your content.
- **Hashtags and Engagement**: Incorporate relevant hashtags to increase your content's visibility. Engage with your audience by responding to comments and DMs, and consider collaborating with others to expand your reach.
- **Analytics Tools**: If you're using Instagram for business, take advantage of Instagram Insights to analyse your audience's behaviour, engagement metrics, and the performance of your posts.

3. TikTok

- **Content Creation**: TikTok is all about creativity and short-form video content. Experiment with trends, challenges, and sound clips to create engaging videos that resonate with the platform's audience.
- **Editing Features**: Utilise TikTok's editing tools, filters, and effects to enhance your videos. Captivating content is more likely to be shared and go viral.
- **Community Guidelines**: Familiarise yourself with TikTok's community guidelines to ensure your content complies with platform standards, promoting a positive experience for all users.

Managing Notifications and Staying Focused

In a world filled with constant notifications, managing alerts from social media and communication apps is vital to maintaining focus and productivity. Here are strategies for effective notification management:

1. Customise Notification Settings

- **Selective Notifications**: Instead of allowing all notifications, customise settings for each app to receive only essential alerts. For instance, enable notifications for direct messages but mute notifications for non-essential updates.
- **Use Do Not Disturb Mode**: Utilise the "Do Not Disturb" feature on your devices during designated focus times. This allows you to concentrate on tasks without distractions from incoming notifications.

2. Schedule Social Media Time

- **Designate Time Blocks**: Allocate specific times during the day for checking social media. This approach helps you manage your time effectively and prevents aimless scrolling.
- **Use App Limiters**: Consider using apps or built-in features on your devices to set limits on your social media usage. These

tools can help you stay accountable and reduce overall screen time.

3. Practice Mindfulness

- **Be Present**: When using social media or engaging in online communication, practice mindfulness by being fully present. Focus on the content you're engaging with and avoid multitasking.
- **Limit Distractions**: Create a designated workspace free from distractions when working on tasks that require concentration. This helps improve productivity and reduces the urge to check notifications.

Video Conferencing Tools: Zoom, Teams, and Skype Basics

With remote work and online meetings becoming the norm, mastering video conferencing tools is essential for effective communication. This section explores the basics of popular platforms like Zoom, Microsoft Teams, and Skype.

1. Zoom

- **Setting Up Meetings**: Create and schedule meetings easily within Zoom. Familiarise yourself with features like screen sharing, breakout rooms, and virtual backgrounds to enhance your meetings.
- **Meeting Etiquette**: Arrive on time, mute your microphone when not speaking, and use the chat function for questions or comments during presentations. Maintain eye contact by looking into the camera when speaking.
- **Recording Features**: Zoom allows you to record meetings for later review. Always inform participants before recording to respect their privacy.

2. Microsoft Teams

- **Collaboration Tools**: Microsoft Teams integrates with other Microsoft 365 applications, allowing for seamless collaboration on projects. Use the chat function for quick communication and file sharing.
- **Channel Organization**: Organise your workspace using channels for different topics or projects, helping to keep conversations focused and relevant.
- **Video and Audio Settings**: Test your audio and video settings before meetings to ensure a smooth experience. Adjust background settings to minimise distractions during video calls.

3. Skype

- **Personal and Professional Use**: Skype is versatile for personal calls and professional meetings. Use it to make voice or video calls and send instant messages.
- **Screen Sharing**: Share your screen during calls for effective collaboration. This

feature is useful for presentations or troubleshooting issues together.

- **Chat History**: Skype allows you to save chat history, enabling you to reference previous conversations and decisions easily.

Safe and Effective Texting and Email Etiquette

Effective communication through texting and email requires understanding proper etiquette to convey your message clearly and respectfully.

1. Texting Etiquette

- **Be Clear and Concise**: Keep your messages short and to the point. Use proper grammar and punctuation to avoid misunderstandings.
- **Respect Response Times**: Understand that not everyone can respond immediately. Avoid sending multiple messages in quick succession if you don't receive a reply right away.

- **Use Emojis Wisely**: Emojis can enhance your messages but use them judiciously. Overuse can come across as unprofessional or diminish the seriousness of your message.

2. Email Etiquette

- **Use a Professional Email Address**: When communicating in professional settings, use an email address that reflects your name or business rather than a casual one.
- **Craft a Clear Subject Line**: A well-written subject line helps the recipient understand the purpose of your email. Make it specific and relevant to the content.
- **Begin with a Greeting**: Start your emails with a polite greeting, addressing the recipient by name. This sets a positive tone for your message.
- **Proofread Before Sending**: Always proofread your emails for typos, grammatical errors, and clarity. A

well-crafted email demonstrates
professionalism and attention to detail.

Chapter 8: Mastering Mobile Devices

Mobile devices have revolutionised the way we communicate, work, and interact with the world around us. Understanding how to effectively use these devices, particularly smartphones, can enhance your productivity and enrich your digital experiences. This chapter focuses on mastering mobile devices by exploring the key differences between iPhone and Android, top apps to improve your mobile experience, tips for extending battery life, and strategies for managing storage on your phone.

iPhone vs. Android: Key Differences

When choosing a smartphone, the iPhone and Android platforms are the most popular options. Understanding their differences can help you make an informed decision based on your needs.

1. Operating System

- **iOS**: Apple's iOS operating system is known for its smooth performance and user-friendly interface. iPhones receive regular updates, ensuring users have access to the latest features and security improvements. The iOS ecosystem is tightly controlled, which enhances security and reliability but limits customization options.

- **Android**: Android, developed by Google, is an open-source operating system that offers a more customizable user experience. Users can choose from various device manufacturers (Samsung, Google, OnePlus, etc.) and customise their home screens, app layouts, and settings. Android users often have access to a wider range of apps and widgets.

2. App Store vs. Google Play Store

- **App Store**: Apple's App Store features a curated selection of apps, ensuring quality and security. However, it may have stricter guidelines for app submissions, potentially limiting the availability of certain applications.
- **Google Play Store**: The Google Play Store has a broader selection of apps, including many free options. However, the open nature of Android means that users may encounter less regulated apps, requiring more diligence in choosing safe downloads.

3. Hardware and Device Variety

- **iPhone**: Apple's iPhones have a consistent design and hardware quality, which contributes to their premium feel.

However, options are limited to Apple's lineup, typically available in a few models each year.

- **Android**: With Android, users can choose from a vast array of devices across different price points, sizes, and features. This variety allows for greater flexibility in selecting a device that meets specific needs.

4. Integration with Other Devices

- **iOS**: If you already use Apple products, such as a MacBook or iPad, an iPhone seamlessly integrates with these devices. Features like Handoff, AirDrop, and iCloud synchronisation enhance the ecosystem experience.
- **Android**: Android devices may not have the same level of integration with non-Google products, but they work well with various third-party applications and services, allowing for a more diverse tech environment.

Top Apps to Improve Your Mobile Experience

To get the most out of your smartphone, consider downloading the following categories of apps that can significantly enhance your daily experience:

1. Productivity Apps

- **Todoist**: A powerful task management app that helps you organise tasks and projects with ease, enabling you to track deadlines and collaborate with others.
- **Evernote**: A versatile note-taking app that allows you to create notes, save web articles, and organise your ideas across different devices.

2. Communication Apps

- **WhatsApp**: A widely-used messaging app that offers free texting, voice, and video calls, making it easy to stay in touch with friends and family around the world.

- **Slack**: Ideal for team communication, Slack enables users to organise conversations into channels, making collaboration and information sharing seamless.

3. Fitness and Health Apps

- **MyFitnessPal**: This app helps track your food intake, exercise, and overall wellness goals, promoting healthier lifestyle choices.
- **Headspace**: A meditation app that guides users through mindfulness exercises, helping reduce stress and improve mental well-being.

4. Travel and Navigation Apps

- **Google Maps**: A powerful navigation tool that provides real-time traffic updates, directions, and local business information.
- **TripIt**: An itinerary management app that organises your travel plans in one place,

making it easy to access your itinerary on
the go.

5. Entertainment Apps

- **Spotify**: A music streaming app that
  provides access to millions of songs,
  curated playlists, and podcasts.
- **Netflix**: A leading streaming service
  offering a wide array of movies and TV
  shows, allowing you to enjoy
  entertainment anytime, anywhere.

Extending Battery Life and Managing Power Settings

Battery life is a crucial aspect of mobile device
usage. With the right strategies, you can extend
the battery life of your smartphone and make the
most of its power settings.

1. Adjust Brightness and Display Settings

- **Lower Screen Brightness**: Reducing
  your screen brightness can significantly
  conserve battery life. Most devices allow

you to adjust brightness automatically based on ambient light conditions.

- **Screen Timeout**: Set a shorter screen timeout duration to ensure your display turns off quickly when not in use.

2. Optimise App Usage

- **Background App Refresh**: Disable background app refresh for apps that don't need to be constantly updated, which can drain battery life. Both iOS and Android have settings to manage this.
- **Uninstall Unused Apps**: Periodically review your installed apps and remove those you no longer use. Many apps run in the background, consuming battery life.

3. Utilise Battery Saver Modes

- **Battery Saver Mode**: Both iPhone and Android devices offer battery saver modes that limit background activity and reduce performance to extend battery life. Enable this feature when your battery is running low.

- **Low Power Mode (iOS)**: This mode reduces background activity and visual effects to conserve battery life, providing you with an extended usage period when needed.

4. Manage Connectivity Settings

- **Turn Off Wi-Fi and Bluetooth**: When you're not using Wi-Fi or Bluetooth, turn them off to save battery life. Both features can drain your battery even when not actively in use.
- **Airplane Mode**: When in areas with poor reception, consider enabling aeroplane mode. This setting disables all wireless communication, conserving battery life until you can connect again.

Managing Storage on Your Phone

As you use your mobile device, storage can fill up quickly, leading to performance issues and limited space for new apps and media. Implementing effective storage management strategies can help keep your device running smoothly.

1. Assess Storage Usage

- **Check Storage Settings**: Both iOS and Android devices provide tools to check storage usage. Review which apps and files consume the most space to identify areas for cleanup.
- **File Management Apps**: Consider using file management apps (like Files by Google) to identify large files, duplicates, and unused apps for deletion.

2. Offload Unused Apps and Media

- **Delete Unused Apps**: Regularly review your installed apps and delete those you no longer use. Uninstalling apps frees up storage space and can improve device performance.

- **Cloud Storage Solutions**: Utilise cloud storage services like Google Drive, iCloud, or Dropbox to store photos, videos, and documents. This strategy keeps your device free from excess media and allows for easy access across devices.

3. Optimise Media Storage

- **Compress Photos and Videos**: Use built-in features or third-party apps to compress photos and videos before saving them on your device. This helps reduce file size without significantly impacting quality.
- **Manage Downloads**: Regularly clean your downloads folder to remove old files, documents, and media you no longer need.

4. Clear Cache and Temporary Files

- **Clear App Cache**: Over time, apps can accumulate cached data that consumes storage space. Clear app cache through settings to free up space without deleting app data.

- **Temporary Files**: Some apps create temporary files that can be deleted safely. Regularly clearing these can help maintain optimal storage levels.

Chapter 9: Advanced Tips for Power Users

This chapter explores advanced techniques that can enhance your productivity, streamline your workflow, and allow you to customise your computing experience. From automating tasks with IFTTT and Shortcuts to building your own website in minutes, these tips will empower you to take control of your digital environment.

Automating Tasks with IFTTT and Shortcuts

IFTTT (If This Then That) is a web-based service that allows users to create automation workflows between various apps and devices.

Similarly, Apple's **Shortcuts** app offers automation capabilities specifically for iOS users. Understanding how to leverage these tools can save you time and effort by automating repetitive tasks.

1. Understanding IFTTT

- **Setting Up an Account**: Creating an account on IFTTT is quick and straightforward. Once you're logged in, you can explore various applets (pre-made automations) or create your own.
- **Creating Applets**: The IFTTT platform operates on a simple premise: "If this happens, then do that." For example, you could set up an applet that automatically saves any photo you post on Instagram to your Dropbox.
- **Exploring Integrations**: IFTTT supports numerous services, from social media platforms to smart home devices. Explore different integrations to find the ones that fit your lifestyle or workflow.

2. Using Shortcuts on iOS

- **Creating a Shortcut**: Open the Shortcuts app on your iPhone or iPad, and tap the "+" icon to create a new shortcut. You can choose from a variety of actions, such as sending a message, setting a timer, or getting directions.
- **Scripting and Automation**: Use the scripting features to create more complex shortcuts. For example, you can combine multiple actions, such as turning on your lights, adjusting the thermostat, and playing your favourite music, all with a single command.
- **Siri Integration**: One of the most powerful features of Shortcuts is its integration with Siri. You can assign custom phrases to your shortcuts, enabling you to automate tasks hands-free.

Customising Your Computer with Scripts and Extensions

Power users often customise their computing environment to increase efficiency and personalise their user experience. Scripting and browser extensions are excellent ways to achieve this.

1. Scripting for Automation

- **Using Shell Scripts**: For users on macOS or Linux, shell scripting can automate repetitive tasks. A shell script can execute a series of commands at once, such as backing up files or batch renaming images.
- **PowerShell on Windows**: Windows users can utilise PowerShell scripts to automate tasks, manage system configurations, and perform batch operations. PowerShell's rich scripting capabilities make it a powerful tool for advanced users.
- **Python and Other Languages**: If you're comfortable with programming, consider using languages like Python or JavaScript to automate tasks on your computer. Python, in particular, has libraries that can

interface with APIs, manipulate files, and automate web browsing.

2. Browser Extensions for Enhanced Productivity

- **Ad Blockers**: Extensions like AdBlock Plus or uBlock Origin enhance your browsing experience by blocking unwanted advertisements and speeding up page load times.
- **Password Managers**: Password management extensions, such as LastPass or 1Password, can help you securely store and auto-fill your passwords, making it easier to manage your online accounts.
- **Productivity Tools**: Extensions like Todoist for task management or Grammarly for writing assistance can integrate directly into your browser, helping you stay organised and productive while you work online.

Using Virtual Machines and Remote Desktops

Virtual machines (VMs) and remote desktop services provide flexibility and access to different operating systems and environments without needing additional hardware.

1. Virtual Machines

- **What is a Virtual Machine?**: A virtual machine is a software-based emulation of a computer that runs an operating system within another operating system. This allows you to run Windows on a Mac or test different Linux distributions on a Windows machine.
- **Setting Up a VM**: Use software like **VirtualBox** or **VMware** to create and manage your virtual machines. You can install multiple operating systems, allowing you to test software, run specific applications, or create a sandbox environment for development.
- **Benefits of Using VMs**: Virtual machines are useful for software development, testing, and learning new operating systems. They allow you to create isolated

environments that won't affect your main system, making them ideal for experimentation.

2. Remote Desktops

- **Understanding Remote Desktop**: Remote desktop services allow you to access and control another computer over the internet. This is useful for accessing your work computer from home or providing tech support to others.
- **Setting Up Remote Desktop**: For Windows, use the built-in Remote Desktop Connection tool. For macOS, apps like **Microsoft Remote Desktop** can help you connect to a remote Windows machine.
- **Remote Access Tools**: Third-party applications like **TeamViewer** or **AnyDesk** provide remote access capabilities and additional features such as file sharing and session recording.

How to Build Your Own Website in Minutes

Building a website is no longer a daunting task reserved for experienced developers. With modern tools and platforms, anyone can create a professional-looking site in just a few minutes.

1. Choose a Website Builder

- **Popular Platforms**: Use website builders like **Wix**, **Squarespace**, or **WordPress.com**. These platforms offer user-friendly interfaces, allowing you to create websites without any coding knowledge.
- **Templates and Customization**: Website builders provide numerous templates that cater to different industries and styles. Choose a template that resonates with your vision and customise it to suit your brand.

2. Set Up Your Domain and Hosting

- **Domain Name**: Choose a memorable domain name that reflects your website's purpose. Many website builders include domain registration services, simplifying the process.
- **Hosting Options**: If you choose a platform like WordPress.org, you'll need to select a hosting provider. Services like **Bluehost** or **SiteGround** offer affordable hosting plans with easy WordPress installations.

3. Add Content and Launch

- **Create Engaging Content**: Populate your website with engaging and relevant content. Use high-quality images, videos, and well-written text to capture your audience's attention.
- **SEO Basics**: Familiarise yourself with basic SEO (Search Engine Optimization) principles to help your website rank higher in search engine results. Use keywords in your content, optimise your images, and create descriptive page titles.

134

- **Launch Your Website**: After reviewing your site for functionality and appearance, hit the publish button! Share your new website with friends, family, and social media to attract visitors.

Chapter 10: Staying Updated in a Rapidly Changing Tech World

This chapter explains the importance of keeping up with tech news and trends, acquiring essential skills for the future, maintaining your software and devices, and understanding the implications of artificial intelligence and automation. By the end of this chapter, you'll be equipped with the knowledge and tools to thrive in this dynamic landscape.

Following Tech News and Trends

1. Importance of Staying Informed

The technology landscape is ever-changing, with new innovations and updates emerging regularly. Staying informed allows you to make better decisions, whether for personal use, professional development, or investment opportunities. Understanding current trends can help you identify potential career paths, improve your skills, and enhance your digital literacy.

2. Reliable Sources for Tech News

- **Tech Websites and Blogs**: Websites like **TechCrunch**, **Wired**, and **The Verge** provide in-depth coverage of the latest tech developments, product reviews, and industry analysis. Following these platforms will help you stay abreast of emerging technologies and trends.
- **Podcasts and YouTube Channels**: There are numerous tech-related podcasts and YouTube channels that offer insights and

discussions on the latest tech news. Programs like **Reply All** and YouTube channels like **MKBHD** provide engaging content that can help you stay updated while on the go.

- **News Aggregators**: Utilise news aggregation apps like **Feedly** or **Flipboard** to curate tech news from multiple sources. This allows you to personalise your news feed, ensuring you receive information that is relevant and interesting to you.

3. Networking and Community Engagement

- **Tech Meetups and Conferences**: Attend tech meetups, webinars, and industry conferences to connect with professionals and enthusiasts in the field. These events often feature keynote speakers and workshops, providing valuable insights into the future of technology.
- **Online Communities**: Join online forums and communities like **Reddit** or **Stack Overflow** to engage in discussions, ask

questions, and share knowledge. These platforms can be excellent resources for learning from others and staying updated on the latest developments.

Essential Tech Skills for the Future

1. Importance of Continuous Learning

As technology evolves, so do the skills required to navigate it effectively. Continuous learning is essential for remaining relevant in the job market and adapting to new tools and platforms.

2. Key Skills to Develop

- **Coding and Programming**: Basic programming knowledge can enhance your problem-solving skills and improve your employability. Languages like Python, JavaScript, and SQL are widely used and can open doors to various tech-related careers.
- **Data Literacy**: In an era dominated by data, being data-literate is crucial. Understanding how to analyse, interpret,

and visualise data can give you a competitive edge. Familiarising yourself with tools like Microsoft Excel, Google Analytics, or data visualisation software like Tableau can be beneficial.

- **Cybersecurity Awareness**: With the increasing frequency of cyberattacks, having a solid understanding of cybersecurity principles is vital. Learn about best practices for protecting your information and recognizing potential threats.

- **Soft Skills**: In addition to technical skills, soft skills such as critical thinking, communication, and adaptability are highly valued in the tech industry. Building these skills will help you collaborate effectively with others and navigate complex problems.

3. Online Learning Platforms

- **MOOCs**: Massive Open Online Courses (MOOCs) offer a flexible way to learn new skills. Platforms like **Coursera**, **edX**, and **Udacity** provide courses from reputable institutions on various tech topics, from programming to data science.

- **YouTube Tutorials**: YouTube is a treasure trove of instructional videos. Channels dedicated to coding, software development, and other tech-related subjects can provide valuable insights and tutorials.

How to Keep Your Software and Devices Updated

1. Importance of Regular Updates

Keeping your software and devices updated is essential for maintaining security, performance, and compatibility with new technologies. Regular updates help protect against vulnerabilities, improve functionality, and enhance user experience.

2. Automatic Updates

- **Enable Automatic Updates**: Most operating systems and applications offer an option to enable automatic updates. Activating this feature ensures that you receive the latest security patches and software improvements without having to remember to check manually.
- **Set a Reminder**: If automatic updates aren't an option, set a reminder to check for updates regularly. Weekly or monthly check-ins can help ensure that you don't miss important updates.

3. Managing Software and Device Updates

- **Software Management**: On Windows, use Windows Update to check for system updates, while Mac users can utilise the App Store to manage updates. Mobile devices, such as iOS and Android, also have built-in update management systems.
- **Third-Party Applications**: For third-party applications, check the developer's website or app store for

updates. Some applications may require you to update them manually.

4. Backup Before Updating

Before performing major updates, it's a good practice to backup your data. Use cloud storage solutions like Google Drive or external hard drives to ensure that your important files are safe in case something goes wrong during the update process.

Staying Ahead with Artificial Intelligence and Automation

1. Understanding AI and Automation

Artificial intelligence and automation are rapidly transforming industries and reshaping the job market. Understanding these technologies and their implications can help you stay ahead in your career and leverage their benefits effectively.

2. Embracing AI Tools

- **AI-Powered Applications**: Familiarise yourself with AI-powered tools that can enhance productivity, such as **ChatGPT** for writing assistance or AI-driven analytics tools for data interpretation.
- **Automation Software**: Explore automation platforms like **Zapier** or **Microsoft Power Automate**, which enable you to create workflows that connect different applications and automate repetitive tasks.

3. Preparing for an AI-Driven Future

- **Adaptability**: Be open to learning and adapting to new technologies as they emerge. Embracing change will help you stay relevant in an evolving job market.
- **Focus on Human Skills**: As AI continues to advance, the demand for uniquely human skills—such as creativity, empathy, and complex problem-solving—will remain high. Cultivating these skills can position you favourably in the job market.

144

4. Ethical Considerations

As AI becomes more integrated into daily life, understanding the ethical implications of its use is crucial. Stay informed about discussions surrounding data privacy, bias in algorithms, and the impact of automation on employment. Engaging with these issues can help you navigate the complexities of an AI-driven world responsibly.

Conclusion: Empower Yourself with Technology

Embracing technology means more than just keeping up with the latest gadgets or trends; it involves leveraging tools and resources to improve our efficiency, enhance our communication, and elevate our overall quality of life.

Summary of Key Tips

Throughout this book, we've explored a variety of topics aimed at empowering you with practical technology tips. Here's a recap of some of the most essential takeaways:

1. **Setting Up Your Devices for Success**:
   - **Optimise Your Devices**: Ensure your smartphones, tablets, and laptops are set up efficiently to improve performance and usability.
   - **Key Apps and Software**: Familiarise yourself with vital applications that enhance your productivity and communication.
2. **Mastering the Basics of the Internet**:
   - **Internet Connectivity**: Understand different ways to connect to the internet, and make sure you're getting the best performance from your service provider.
   - **Safe Browsing**: Develop habits to avoid scams and phishing attempts while surfing the web.
3. **Troubleshooting Common Tech Problems**:

- ○ **Identifying Issues**: Learn how to diagnose slow devices, connectivity issues, and software crashes.
- ○ **Quick Fixes**: Equip yourself with techniques to resolve these problems efficiently.

4. **Enhancing Your Productivity with Technology**:
   - ○ **Utilise Productivity Tools**: Explore apps that can streamline your tasks and improve collaboration in both work and academic settings.
   - ○ **Cloud Storage**: Leverage cloud services for seamless access and sharing of documents and files.

5. **Boosting Your Digital Security and Privacy**:
   - ○ **Stay Secure**: Implement two-factor authentication, manage privacy settings, and regularly back up your data to keep your information safe.
   - ○ **Be Vigilant Against Threats**: Understand how to recognize malware and scams.

6. **Navigating Social Media and Communication**:
   - o **Engage Responsibly**: Use social media platforms wisely, managing notifications to minimise distractions and maintaining effective communication etiquette.
   - o **Video Conferencing**: Get comfortable with tools like Zoom and Teams to connect with others virtually.
7. **Mastering Mobile Devices**:
   - o **Choosing the Right Device**: Know the key differences between iPhone and Android to select the best device for your needs.
   - o **Extend Battery Life**: Use power-saving modes and manage background apps to ensure your device lasts throughout the day.
8. **Advanced Tips for Power Users**:
   - o **Automation**: Explore automation tools like IFTTT to streamline

repetitive tasks and improve workflow.

- ○ **Web Development Basics**: Learn how to build simple websites to establish an online presence.

9. **Staying Updated in a Rapidly Changing Tech World**:
   - ○ **Follow Tech News**: Stay informed about the latest trends and innovations to adapt to the changing landscape.
   - ○ **Continuous Learning**: Develop essential skills to thrive in the future, focusing on both technical abilities and human-centric skills.

Keeping a Healthy Tech-Life Balance

While technology offers a wealth of opportunities, it is essential to maintain a healthy balance between our digital lives and real-world interactions. Over-reliance on technology can lead to stress, anxiety, and a feeling of disconnection from those around us. Here are some strategies to help maintain this balance:

1. **Set Boundaries**:
   - Designate specific times during the day to unplug from devices. This can help reduce stress and improve your mental well-being.
   - Create tech-free zones in your home, such as the dining room or bedroom, to foster family interactions and encourage relaxation.
2. **Mindful Usage**:
   - Be conscious of the time spent on devices and the content you consume. Opt for quality over quantity in both your media consumption and online interactions.
   - Engage in activities that do not involve screens, such as reading, exercising, or spending time outdoors.

3. **Social Interactions**:
   - ○ Prioritise face-to-face interactions whenever possible. These connections are essential for emotional well-being and can help foster stronger relationships.
   - ○ Use technology as a tool to enhance these connections rather than replace them. Video calls, for example, can bridge the gap when distance is a factor.

4. **Reflect and Adjust**:
   - ○ Regularly assess your tech usage and its impact on your life. Make adjustments as needed to ensure that technology remains a helpful tool rather than a source of stress.
   - ○ Encourage open conversations with friends and family about technology use and its effects on well-being.

Next Steps: Building Your Tech Knowledge

Empowering yourself with technology is an ongoing journey. Here are some actionable steps to continue expanding your tech knowledge:

1. **Set Learning Goals**:
   - Identify areas of technology that interest you and set specific goals for learning. This could include mastering a new programming language, becoming proficient in data analysis, or exploring emerging technologies like AI or blockchain.

2. **Participate in Online Courses**:
   - Utilise online learning platforms such as Coursera, Udemy, or LinkedIn Learning to find courses that match your interests and goals. These resources offer flexibility and can cater to all skill levels.

3. **Engage with Community Resources**:
   - Join local tech meetups, workshops, or community colleges that offer technology courses. Networking

with like-minded individuals can also lead to new opportunities and insights.

4. **Stay Curious**:

   - Maintain a mindset of curiosity and openness to new ideas. Follow technology blogs, listen to podcasts, and read books that challenge your thinking and broaden your perspective.

5. **Practice Regularly**:

   - Apply your newly acquired skills in real-world scenarios. Whether it's building a website, creating a blog, or exploring programming projects, practical experience is crucial for reinforcing your learning.

Appendix: Quick Reference Guides

This appendix serves as a handy reference for common tasks, shortcuts, and resources to further your learning and troubleshooting skills.

Common Keyboard Shortcuts for Windows and Mac

Mastering keyboard shortcuts can greatly enhance your productivity by reducing reliance on the mouse and speeding up common tasks. Here's a list of some of the most useful shortcuts for both Windows and Mac users:

Windows Shortcuts

- **Ctrl + C**: Copy the selected item.
- **Ctrl + V**: Paste the copied item.
- **Ctrl + X**: Cut the selected item.

- **Ctrl** + **Z**: Undo the last action.
- **Ctrl** + **A**: Select all items in a document or window.
- **Alt** + **Tab**: Switch between open applications.
- **Windows Key** + **D**: Show or hide the desktop.
- **Windows Key** + **L**: Lock your computer.
- **Ctrl** + **Shift** + **Esc**: Open Task Manager directly.
- **Windows Key** + **E**: Open File Explorer.

Mac Shortcuts

- **Command** (⌘) + **C**: Copy the selected item.
- **Command** (⌘) + **V**: Paste the copied item.
- **Command** (⌘) + **X**: Cut the selected item.
- **Command** (⌘) + **Z**: Undo the last action.
- **Command** (⌘) + **A**: Select all items.
- **Command** (⌘) + **Tab**: Switch between open applications.

156

- **Command (⌘) + Space**: Open Spotlight search.
- **Command (⌘) + H**: Hide the current application.
- **Command (⌘) + Option + Esc**: Force quit an application.
- **Control (⌃) + Command (⌘) + Q**: Lock your Mac.

Essential Smartphone Gestures

Smartphones come equipped with a range of gestures that simplify navigation and enhance user experience. Familiarising yourself with these gestures can improve your efficiency and speed when using mobile devices.

For iPhone Users

- **Swipe Down**: Access Notification Centre.
- **Swipe Up**: Open Control Center (from the bottom of the screen) or go to the Home

screen (from the bottom edge on newer models).

- **Pinch**: Zoom in or out on photos, maps, or websites.
- **Tap and Hold**: Access options like "Copy," "Paste," and app-specific menus.
- **Swipe Left/Right**: Navigate between apps or screens.

For Android Users

- **Swipe Down**: Access Quick Settings and Notifications.
- **Swipe Up**: Open the app drawer.
- **Pinch**: Zoom in or out in apps, including the map and photo viewers.
- **Long Press**: Access additional options or context menus for apps and items.
- **Two-Finger Swipe**: Zoom in or out in supported apps.

Must-Know Commands for Tech Troubleshooting

Sometimes, technology can be unpredictable, and knowing key commands can help troubleshoot issues effectively. Here's a compilation of commands that can assist with troubleshooting various tech problems:

Windows Commands

- **Windows Key + R**: Open the Run dialog box for quick access to programs and utilities.
- **ipconfig**: Check your IP address and network configuration in Command Prompt.
- **ping [website]**: Test your internet connection to a specific website.
- **sfc /scannow**: Run the System File Checker to scan and repair corrupted system files.
- **chkdsk**: Check the disk for errors and repair them (type in Command Prompt).

Mac Commands

- **Command (⌘) + Option (⌥) + Esc**: Force quit an unresponsive application.
- **Activity Monitor**: Access through Applications > Utilities to view running processes and resource usage.
- **Terminal**: Use various commands for network troubleshooting (e.g., ping, traceroute).
- **Reset NVRAM**: Restart your Mac and hold Command (⌘) + Option (⌥) + P + R until you hear the startup sound twice.
- **Disk Utility**: Access through Applications > Utilities to check and repair disk issues.

Resources for Further Learning (Websites, YouTube Channels, Podcasts)

Continuing your tech education is vital in an ever-evolving digital landscape. Below is a list of valuable resources, including websites, YouTube channels, and podcasts that can provide you with in-depth knowledge and the latest updates in technology.

Websites

- **TechRadar**: Offers comprehensive reviews and news about the latest technology products and trends.
- **CNET**: A great resource for technology news, reviews, and how-to guides.
- **Lifehacker**: Focuses on tips and tricks to improve productivity and make life easier through technology.
- **Wired**: Covers the intersection of technology, culture, and politics, providing insights on how tech influences society.

YouTube Channels

- **TechGumbo**: Offers reviews and tech tips for a variety of gadgets and software.
- **Linus Tech Tips**: Features hardware reviews, build guides, and tech news.

- **The Verge**: Covers technology, science, art, and culture, offering insightful commentary and analysis.
- **TED-Ed**: Provides educational videos on a range of topics, including technology.

Podcasts

- **Reply All**: A podcast about the internet, featuring stories about how technology impacts our lives.
- **This Week in Tech (TWiT)**: Discusses the latest technology news and developments with industry experts.
- **The Daily**: Although not strictly tech-focused, it covers significant news stories, including those related to technology and innovation.
- **Accidental Tech Podcast**: A tech podcast discussing the latest trends, gadgets, and software from a developer's perspective.

Glossary of Terms

1. Algorithm: A set of rules or calculations to solve a problem or complete a task.

2. API (Application Programming Interface): A set of protocols for building and integrating application software.

3. Bandwidth: The maximum data transfer rate of a network or internet connection.

4. Bluetooth: A wireless technology standard for exchanging data over short distances.

5. Browser: A software application used to access and navigate the internet.

6. Cache: A storage area that temporarily holds frequently accessed data for faster retrieval.

7. Cloud Computing: Storing and accessing data and programs over the internet instead of on local computers.

8. CPU (Central Processing Unit): The primary component of a computer that performs calculations and processes instructions.

9. CSS (Cascading Style Sheets): A style sheet language used for describing the presentation of a document written in HTML.

10. Data Encryption: The process of converting information into a code to prevent unauthorised access.

11. Database: An organised collection of structured information stored electronically.

12. DNS (Domain Name System): The system that translates domain names into IP addresses.

13. Email Client: A software application for accessing and managing a user's email.

14. Firewall: A network security system that monitors and controls incoming and outgoing network traffic.

15. Firmware: Permanent software programmed into a read-only memory of a device.

16. GPU (Graphics Processing Unit): A specialised processor designed to accelerate graphics rendering.

17. HTML (HyperText Markup Language): The standard markup language for creating web pages.

18. HTTP (HyperText Transfer Protocol):
The protocol used for transferring hypertext
requests and information on the internet.

**19. HTTPS (HyperText Transfer Protocol
Secure):** A secure version of HTTP that
encrypts data exchanged between the browser
and server.

20. IoT (Internet of Things): A network of
physical devices connected to the internet,
enabling them to collect and exchange data.

21. IP Address: A unique string of numbers
assigned to each device connected to a
network that uses the Internet Protocol for
communication.

22. ISP (Internet Service Provider): A
company that provides access to the internet.

23. Malware: Malicious software designed to
harm, exploit, or otherwise compromise
computers and networks.

24. Phishing: A technique used to trick individuals into revealing sensitive information, often through deceptive emails or websites.

25. Python: A high-level programming language known for its readability and versatility.

26. QR Code (Quick Response Code): A two-dimensional barcode that can be scanned with a smartphone to access information quickly.

27. RAM (Random Access Memory): A type of computer memory that can be accessed randomly; used to store data temporarily.

28. ROM (Read-Only Memory): A type of non-volatile memory that is used to store firmware.

29. Router: A device that forwards data packets between computer networks.

30. SaaS (Software as a Service): A software distribution model in which applications are hosted by a service provider and made available to users over the internet.

31. SEO (Search Engine Optimization): The practice of optimising a website to increase its visibility on search engines.

32. Server: A computer or program that provides data, resources, or services to other computers on a network.

33. SSH (Secure Shell): A protocol for securely accessing network devices over an unsecured network.

34. SSL (Secure Sockets Layer): A protocol for establishing a secure connection between a web server and a browser.

35. Trojan Horse: A type of malware that disguises itself as legitimate software to gain access to a user's system.

36. UI (User Interface): The means by which a user interacts with a computer, software, or application.

37. UX (User Experience): The overall experience a user has when interacting with a product, especially in terms of how easy or pleasing it is to use.

38. VPN (Virtual Private Network): A service that creates a secure connection over the internet, masking your IP address and encrypting your data.

39. Wi-Fi: A technology that allows electronic devices to connect to a wireless local area network (WLAN).

40. XML (eXtensible Markup Language): A markup language that defines a set of rules for encoding documents in a format that is both human-readable and machine-readable.

41. Adware: Software that automatically displays or downloads advertising material.

42. Bloatware: Software that is pre-installed on a device that is often unnecessary and takes up system resources.

43. Browser Extension: A small software module that adds specific functionality to a web browser.

44. Cryptocurrency: A digital currency that uses cryptography for security and operates on a decentralised network.

45. DDoS (Distributed Denial of Service): A cyber attack where multiple compromised systems are used to target a single system, causing disruption.

46. E-commerce: Buying and selling goods or services over the internet.

47. FOMO (Fear of Missing Out): Anxiety that an exciting or interesting event may currently be happening elsewhere.

48. Git: A version control system that allows multiple people to work on code at the same time.

49. Hacker: A person who uses technical skills to gain unauthorised access to systems or networks.

50. Internet Protocol (IP): A set of rules governing the format of data sent over the internet or local network.

51. Java: A high-level programming language used for building platform-independent applications.

52. Keyboard Shortcut: A combination of keys that performs a specific function within software.

53. Load Balancer: A device that distributes network or application traffic across multiple servers.

54. Malware: Software designed to disrupt, damage, or gain unauthorised access to computer systems.

55. NAT (Network Address Translation): A method of remapping an IP address space into another by modifying network address information.

56. Open Source: Software whose source code is available for anyone to inspect, modify, and enhance.

57. Payload: The part of malware that executes the intended malicious action.

58. Queue: A data structure that follows the First In First Out (FIFO) principle.

59. Ransomware: A type of malware that locks or encrypts a user's data and demands payment for its release.

60. SEO (Search Engine Optimization): The practice of optimising a website to rank higher in search engine results.

61. Tethering: Sharing the internet connection of a mobile device with another device, such as a laptop.

62. USB (Universal Serial Bus): A standard for connecting peripherals to a computer.

63. Version Control: A system that records changes to files or sets of files over time so that specific versions can be recalled later.

64. Web Hosting: A service that allows individuals or organisations to post a website on the internet.

65. XML (eXtensible Markup Language): A markup language that defines rules for encoding documents in a format that is both human-readable and machine-readable.

66. Y2K Bug: A computer bug related to the year 2000, where systems that used two-digit year formats faced potential failures.

67. Zero-Day Exploit: A security vulnerability that is exploited before the vendor has issued a fix.

68. Algorithm: A set of rules or a step-by-step procedure for solving a problem.

69. Big Data: Large and complex data sets that traditional data processing software cannot manage.

70. Content Management System (CMS): Software that helps users create, manage, and modify content on a website without needing specialised technical knowledge.

71. Data Mining: The process of discovering patterns and knowledge from large amounts of data.

72. Email Encryption: The method of encoding email messages to protect the content from unauthorised access.

73. Firmware: A type of software that provides low-level control for a device's specific hardware.

74. GitHub: A platform for version control and collaboration, allowing developers to work together on projects.

75. Hyperlink: A link in a digital document that directs the user to another location, such as a different webpage.

76. Intranet: A private network accessible only to an organisation's staff.

77. JavaScript: A programming language commonly used in web development to create interactive effects within web browsers.

78. Keylogger: A type of malware that records keystrokes made by a user.

79. Load Testing: The process of putting demand on a system and measuring its response.

80. Metadata: Data that provides information about other data.

81. Node: A point of intersection or connection in a network.

82. OAuth: An open standard for access delegation commonly used for token-based authentication.

83. PaaS (Platform as a Service): A cloud computing model that provides a platform allowing customers to develop, run, and manage applications.

84. Quality Assurance (QA): A way of preventing errors or defects in manufactured products and avoiding problems when delivering solutions.

85. Remote Desktop: A software that allows a user to connect to a computer in another location.

86. Scripting Language: A programming language used for writing scripts that automate processes.

87. Telemetry: The collection and transmission of data from remote or inaccessible sources.

88. User Acceptance Testing (UAT): A phase of software development where the end users test the software to ensure it meets their needs.

89. Virtual Machine: A software emulation of a physical computer that can run an operating system and applications.

90. Wi-Fi 6: The latest standard for wireless networking, offering faster speeds and improved efficiency.

91. XML Schema: A way to define the structure and data types of XML documents.

92. Yield Management: The process of understanding, anticipating, and influencing consumer behaviour to maximise revenue.

93. Zenith: The highest point; often used in the context of technology to describe the peak of performance or development.

94. A/B Testing: A method of comparing two versions of a webpage or product to determine which one performs better.

95. Byte: A unit of digital information that consists of eight bits.

96. Compiler: A program that converts high-level programming code into machine code.

97. Debugging: The process of identifying and removing errors from computer hardware or software.

98. E-Discovery: The process of seeking, locating, and searching for electronic data for use as evidence in legal cases.

99. Firmware Update: A software update that improves or adds functionality to a device's firmware.

100. Green Computing: Environmentally sustainable computing practices, including energy efficiency and proper disposal of electronic waste.

Tech Made Simple

180

Tech Made Simple

www.ingramcontent.com/pod-product-compliance
Lightning Source LLC
La Vergne TN
LVHW051235050326
832903LV00028B/2417